PRESCHOOL

Student Activity book for Preschool Children (4-5 years of age).
Corresponds to year 1 of the 2-year cycle for Preschoolers.

STUDENT
Year 1

I0086807

These lessons are adapted from material originally published by WordAction Publications.

Preschool 1 - Student Activity Worksheets

Published by: Mesoamerica Region Discipleship Ministries
www.discipleship.MesoamericaRegion.org
www.SdmiResources.mesoamericaregion.org

ISBN: 978-1-63580-078-4

All of the scripture verses quoted are from the NIV Bible unless otherwise stated.

Translated into English from Spanish by:
Monte Cyr

Printed in the United States

Table of Contents

JESUS' FAMILY GOES TO EGYPT

My photo book about Jesus.

Jesus was born.

Jesus visited the temple when he was 12 years old.

When Jesus grew he helped many people.

Jesus told the people about the love of God, and he showed that love to Zacchaeus.

His parents took him to Egypt.

Jesus healed a sick girl.

And the child grew and became strong. (Luke 2:40).

God took care of Jesus while he grew.

And the child grew and became strong. (Luke 2:40).

Search in the Cut-Out Section for the figures that correspond to this lesson. Fold the page in the form of an accordion, with the page divided into four sections. Cut out and paste the figures as indicated in the teacher's book.

NAME: _____

We go!

Instructions: Help the children cut their worksheet in half and fold in three parts the section where the drawings of the family of Jesus are shown (see the example).
Ask: Why is Joseph waking up Mary? (Have the children show the corresponding picture). Where are Joseph, Mary and baby Jesus going? (Show the figure and give the opportunity to answer). Why are they leaving? (Extend the sheet and point to the drawing on the back). As the children color the drawing of Jesus' family, remind them that God protected little Jesus from danger. He helped Joseph escape with his family to Egypt. God cared for Jesus, and also takes care of you.

Dear Parents:
Encourage your child to use this activity sheet to tell you about the journey of Jesus' family to Egypt (Matthew 2: 13-15, 19-21). God cared for his son Jesus, and takes care of us as well.

Wake up!

JESUS VISITS THE TEMPLE

Jesus grew. Jesus was in the temple.

Cut out and paste the figure of Jesus in the Temple

Cut out the figure of Jesus as a boy and paste it here.

Cut out the small red statement below that Jesus grew... and paste it here.

Jesus is the Son of God. He helps people know God.

Cut out and paste this over the figure of Jesus. (See example on next page.).

Jesus grew.

Jesus was in the temple.

7

Instructions: Explain that this is a game of questions and answers. They must keep the figure of Jesus covered while you ask the questions. When they have the answer, they must lift the flap to show Jesus and answer aloud. Stand in the center and ask your students: How old was Jesus in today's story? (Allow them to answer.) Why are Mary and Joseph looking for Jesus? Where was Jesus? What was he doing in the temple? When concluding, congratulate them for their participation, and praise them for wanting to learning. Emphasize that Jesus was the Son of God and grew in stature and knowledge each day. He helped others to learn about God. Jesus loves us and also wants to help us to know God more.

Dear Parents:

Today your child learned about baby Jesus and his growth. In our Bible story, we saw that Jesus was twelve years old when he went to visit the temple. Use the questions on this sheet to talk with your child about this special visit.

Talk about the joy you experience when you go to church. Encourage him/her to expresses their feelings about being in the House of God. Tell him/her that God wants to help them grow, and that He loves them.

JESUS HEALS A SICK GIRL

"And the child grew and became strong." (Luke 2:40)

Instructions: Have your students to cut out the four boxes. You may need to help them with this activity. Then have student mix up their cards, so that they are disordered. Explain that they should put their cards in the correct order according to what they learned in the Bible story today. Check that they have done well; If not, clarify any questions that may arise and emphasize that Jesus takes care of people. In this case he took care of the sick girl and her family. Jesus healed her because he is the Son of God and only he does what no one else can do. Say: Jesus also takes care of you and will always be with you. Ask your students the following questions and let them respond:

- **How does Jesus care for you?**
- **How does Jesus show his love for others?**
- **How do your parents show you their love?**

Dear Parents:

Jesus, the Son of God, could do everything without limitations. He helped others and healed a girl who was very sick (Luke 8: 40-42, 49-56). Talk with your child about Jesus, our friend. He takes care of us when we are sick; We can tell him how we feel. Encourage your child to tell you the Bible story, using the picture cards and putting them in the right order.

JESUS VISITS ZACCHAEUS

Zacheaus, come down from there!

"And the child grew and became strong."
(Luke 2:40)

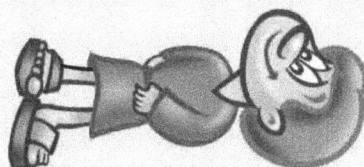

Dear Parents:

This is the last lesson that tells us about how Jesus grew. This week we talked about Zacchaeus (Luke 19:1-9). Ask your child to use the activity that they did in the class to tell you what happened when Zacchaeus met Jesus.

Instructions: Cut out the figures of Zacchaeus. Put tape on the back of the figures to stick them on and take them off easily. Ask the children to move the figures of Zacchaeus and place them in the correct place as they tell what they learned in today's class.

Ask them:

• Why did Zacchaeus climb the tree?
• What did Jesus do when he saw him?
• What did Zacchaeus do after meeting Jesus?

Tell them: Zacchaeus learned that God loved him. God also loves us!

JESUS HEALS AN OLD WOMAN

A **miracle** is something special that only Jesus can do because he is the Son of God.

MY NAME:

Give all your worries to God, because he cares for you. (1 Peter 5:7)

Jesus heals a grandmother

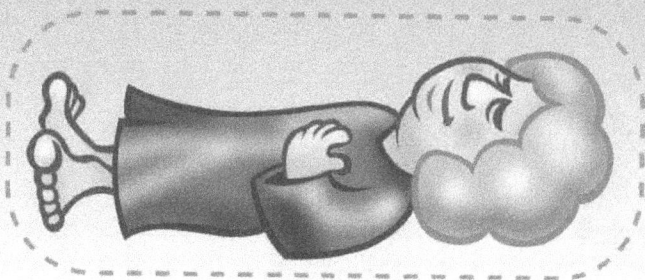

- Cut out the figure of the grandmother, and glue it onto a piece of cardboard so that it can remain vertical.
- Carefully cut out the two lines marked in the picture.

13

Dear Parent:

Our Word of Faith for the next four weeks is "miracle." A miracle is something special that Jesus can do because he is the Son of God. The following four stories focus on the miracles of Jesus.

- Jesus heals an old lady (Mark 1:29-31).

- Jesus helps a fisherman (Luke 5:1-11).

- Jesus calms the storm (Mathew 8:23-27).

- Jesus feeds the multitude (John 6:1-14).

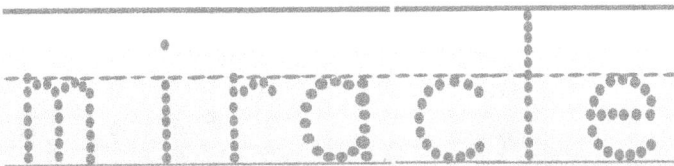

A **miracle** is something special that only Jesus can do because he is the son of God.

Help your child to follow the line of dots and trace the word "miracle" with a pencil or crayon.

JESUS HELPS A FISHERMAN

A miracle is something special that only Jesus can do because he is the son of God.

THE GREAT FISHING TRIP

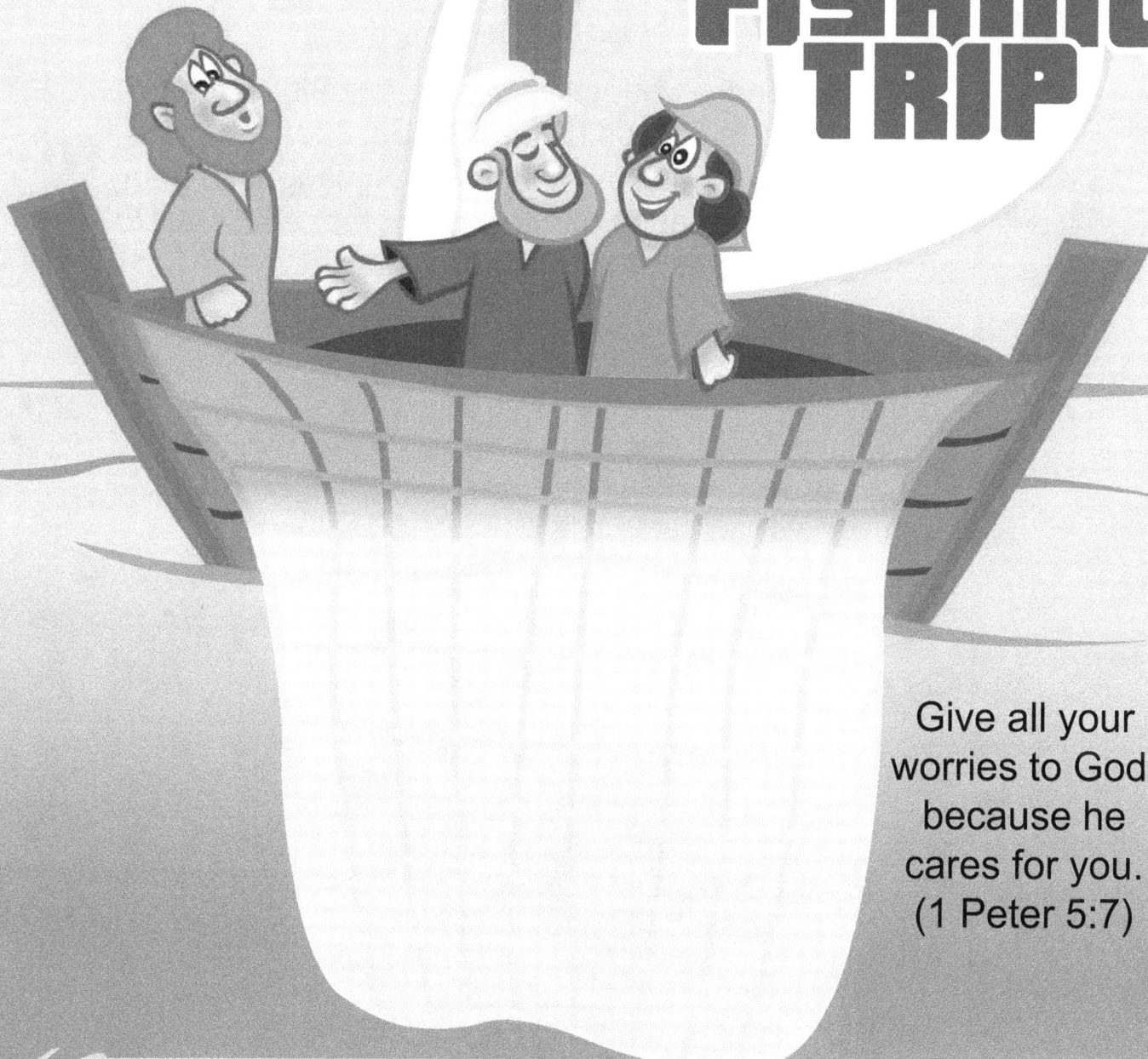

Give all your worries to God, because he cares for you.
(1 Peter 5:7)

MY NAME:

15

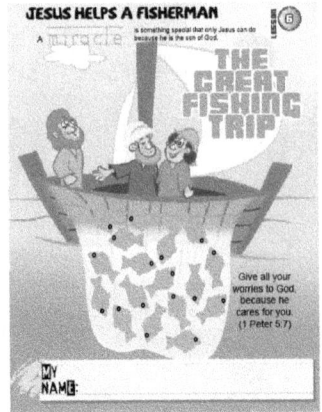

JESUS HELPS A FISHERMAN

A MIRACLE

is something special that only Jesus can do because he is the son of God.

THE GREAT FISHING TRIP

Give all your worries to God, because he cares for you. (1 Peter 5:7)

MY NAME:

Dear Parents:

Today your child learned the Bible story of when Jesus helped Simon, the fisherman, catch fish in his net. Simon caught so many fish that he had to call another boat over to help him with his great catch. (Luke 5:1-11).

JESUS CALMS THE STORM

A **miracle** is something special that only Jesus can do because he is the son of God.

Give all your worries to God, because he cares for you.
(1 Peter 5:7)

MY NAME:

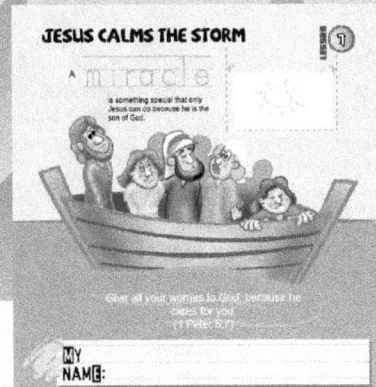

JESUS CALMS THE STORM — LESSON 7

A miracle is something special that only Jesus can do because he is the son of God.

Give all your worries to God, because he cares for you.
(1 Peter 5:7)

MY NAME:

JESUS CALMS THE STORM — LESSON 7

A miracle is something special that only Jesus can do because he is the son of God.

Give all your worries to God, because he cares for you.
(1 Peter 5:7)

MY NAME:

JESUS CALMS THE STORM — LESSON 7

A miracle is something special that only Jesus can do because he is the son of God.

Give all your worries to God, because he cares for you.
(1 Peter 5:7)

MY NAME:

Dear Parent:

Jesus, the Son of God, can do what others can't. In today's Bible story (Matthew 8:23-27), Jesus ordered the wind, waves, and the rain to be calm. His disciples were amazed at this miracle. Talk about this amazing fact with your child, telling them the story of Jesus calming the storm again.

JESUS FEEDS THE CROWD

FISH & BREAD

_____ is something special that only Jesus can do because He is the son of God.

A _ _ _ _ _ _ _

Give all your worries to God, because he cares for you. (1 Peter 5:7).

MY NAME:

19

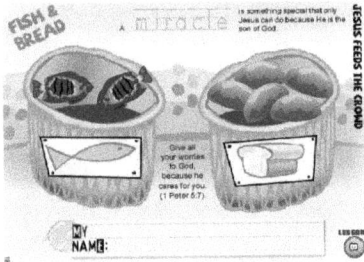

Jesus did

miracles

Dear Parents:

Today your child learned about one of the great miracles that Jesus did. He fed more than 5000 people with only 2 fish and 5 loaves of bread (John 6:1-14). While your child puts the pictures of the bread in the 12 baskets, remind them of the miracles they have learned about in the previous 4 weeks.

- **Jesus healed the old woman**
- **Jesus calmed the storm**
- **The great catch of fish**
- **The feeding of the crowd**

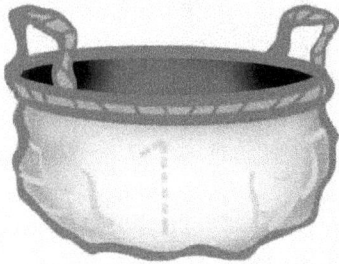

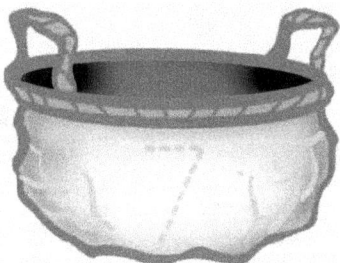

God shows his love through parents.

MY NAME:

The lessons of this unit will help children understand that God shows us his love through parents, grandparents, friends of the church and through Jesus. Our Word of Faith will teach them the importance of knowing that God loves everyone equally. He is the only one that can make the heavens, the earth, and all that exists. This activity will hep you reinforce the Word of Faith to your child during the week.

G o d shows his love through parents.

GOD

God

shows his love through grandparents.

Timothy and his grandmother

MY NAME:

Today's lesson was: "God shows his love through grandparents." Help your child draw a picture, or glue/paste a photo, of their grandparent(s) or some familiar older adult(s) in the space provided. Give thanks to God for showing us his love through grandparents and older people.

GOD

shows his love through brothers and sisters of the church.

MY NAME:

Today's lesson was: "God shows his love through the brothers and sisters of the church." Ask your child to draw what he/she likes to do the most with brothers and sisters of the church. Encourage him/her to enjoy their friendships with them.

God **shows his love through Jesus.**

MY NAME:

Have the child glue the picture onto a piece of cardboard or stiff paper, color the picture if they want, and
then cut out the pieces. Tell them to put the puzzle together at home, and remember the Bible story.

JESUS RESURRECTS LAZARUS

Lazarus' labyrinth

Jesus Lives

You are the Messiah, the Son of the living God.

(Matthew 16:16)

MY NAME:

29

"Jesus Lives!" is our Word of Faith for the following 5 weeks. We celebrate the resurrection of Christ during Easter Week, with a special party in our churches because we remember that Jesus, the Son of God, lives forever. Help your child experience the joy of this time and the importance that it has for his/her spiritual growth.

Each lesson speaks to us about Jesus' life and ministry on earth. Talk with your child about the way in which Jesus can impact their life.

Jesus resurrects Lazarus	John 11:1-23, 34-45
Jesus heals the blind man	Mark 10:46-52
Jesus talk to Peter	Matthew 16:13-116
Jesus goes to Jerusalem	Matthew 21:1-11, 15-16
Jesus lives!	John 20:1-18

Jesus Lives

Draw a picture of what you imagine Lazarus looked like when he came out of the tomb.

JESUS HEALS A BLIND MAN

Book of Bartimaeus

You are the Messiah, the Son of the living God. (Matthew 16:16)

Instructions:
1. Color all the figures.
2. Cut out the four boxes.
3. Put the boxes in order from 1-4.
4. Join the four boxes together to form a small book.

Jesus and his disciples traveled a long way. Many people followed them.

Bartimaeus could not see. He was seated beside the road asking for money.

MY NAME:

Jesus healed Bartimaeus! Now he could see and he was very happy!

Bartimaeus needed Jesus' help, and Jesus gave him his sight.

Jesus Lives

JESUS TALKS WITH PETER

Jesus Lives

The letter  is special

Jesus

is the Son of God.

MY NAME:

33

Dear Parents: Today your child learned that Jesus is the Son of God. Rejoice with them and celebrate Jesus' resurrection.

Jesus Lives

JESUS

is the Son of God

You are the Messiah, the Son of the living God. (Matthew 16:16)

Decorate the letters with crayons or colored pencils.

JESUS GOES TO JERUSALEM

We worship Jesus!

Jesus Lives

You are the Messiah, the
Son of the living God.
(Matthew 16:16)

MY
NAME:

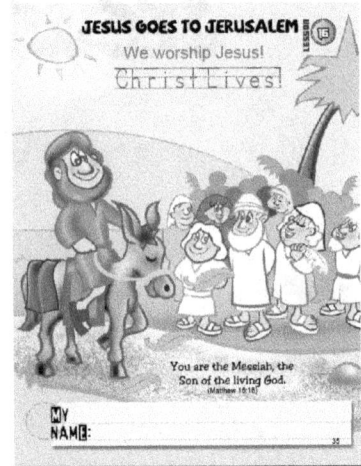

We worship Jesus!

Christ Lives!

You are the Messiah, the
Son of the living God.
(Matthew 16:16)

MY
NAME:

Dear Parents

Today your child experienced the emotions of Jesus' triumphal entrance into Jerusalem. Prepare him/her during the week for the next lesson which will be about Resurrection Sunday.

Jesus Lives

JESUS LIVES!

Jesus Lives

You are the Messiah, the Son of the living God. (Matthew 16:16)

MY NAME:

JESUS LIVES!

ChristLives

You are the Messiah, the Son of the living God. (Matthew 16:16)

MY NAME:

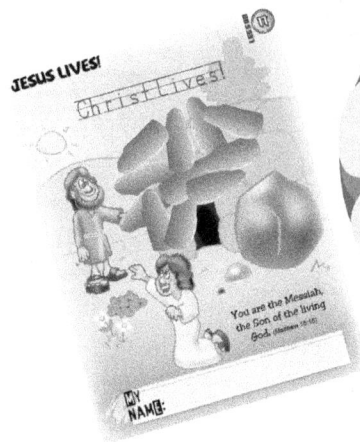

You will need pieces of sandpaper, crepe paper or something else that can help simulate the texture or look of stones. Share them among your students, and help them cover the tomb as shown.

Jesus **is** *Alive!*

Jesus Lives

Dear Parents

Celebrate the joy of the Resurrection with your child during this week, and remember that Jesus, the Son of God, lives forever!!!

GOD MADE THE WORLD

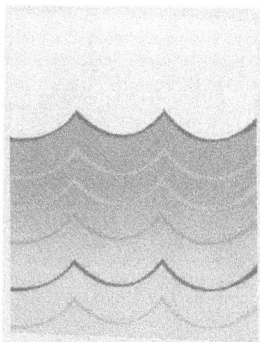

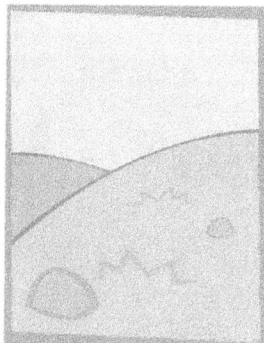

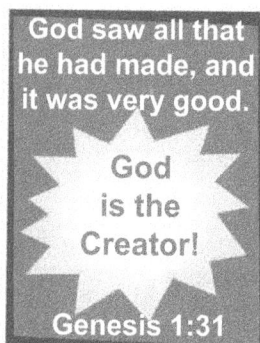

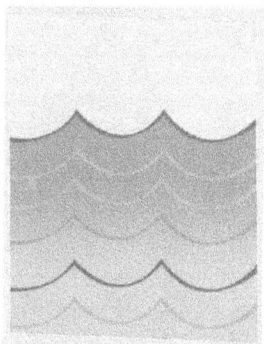

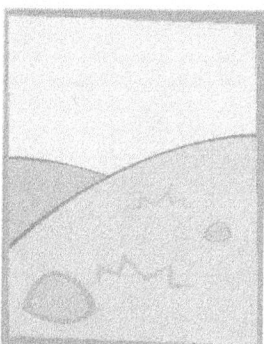

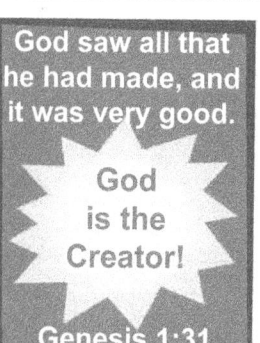

God saw all that he had made, and it was very good.

God is the Creator!

Genesis 1:31

God saw all that he had made, and it was very good.

God is the Creator!

Genesis 1:31

Match Game

Instructions:

1. Allow your students to color the cards, if they would like to. Then help them cut out the cards.
2. Mix up the cards and put them face down on the table.
3. Each child will turn over two cards in order to find the matching pairs. Talk about what the drawings show us about the Bible Story.
4. Keep the cards in a plastic bag so that the children can take them home.

GOD MAKES PEOPLE

God is our **Creator**

God made everything that exists.

What is your name?

God is **Creator**
our

God made everything that exists.

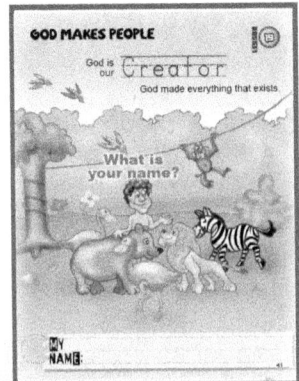

Dear Parents:

Today your child learned that God is the Creator (Genesis 1:27-31; 2:8, 15, 19-20). The Word of Faith is "Creator." God made the world and everything that there is. When he was finished, God made Adam and someone to be his friend - Eve.

Of all the animals that God created, draw your favorite below.

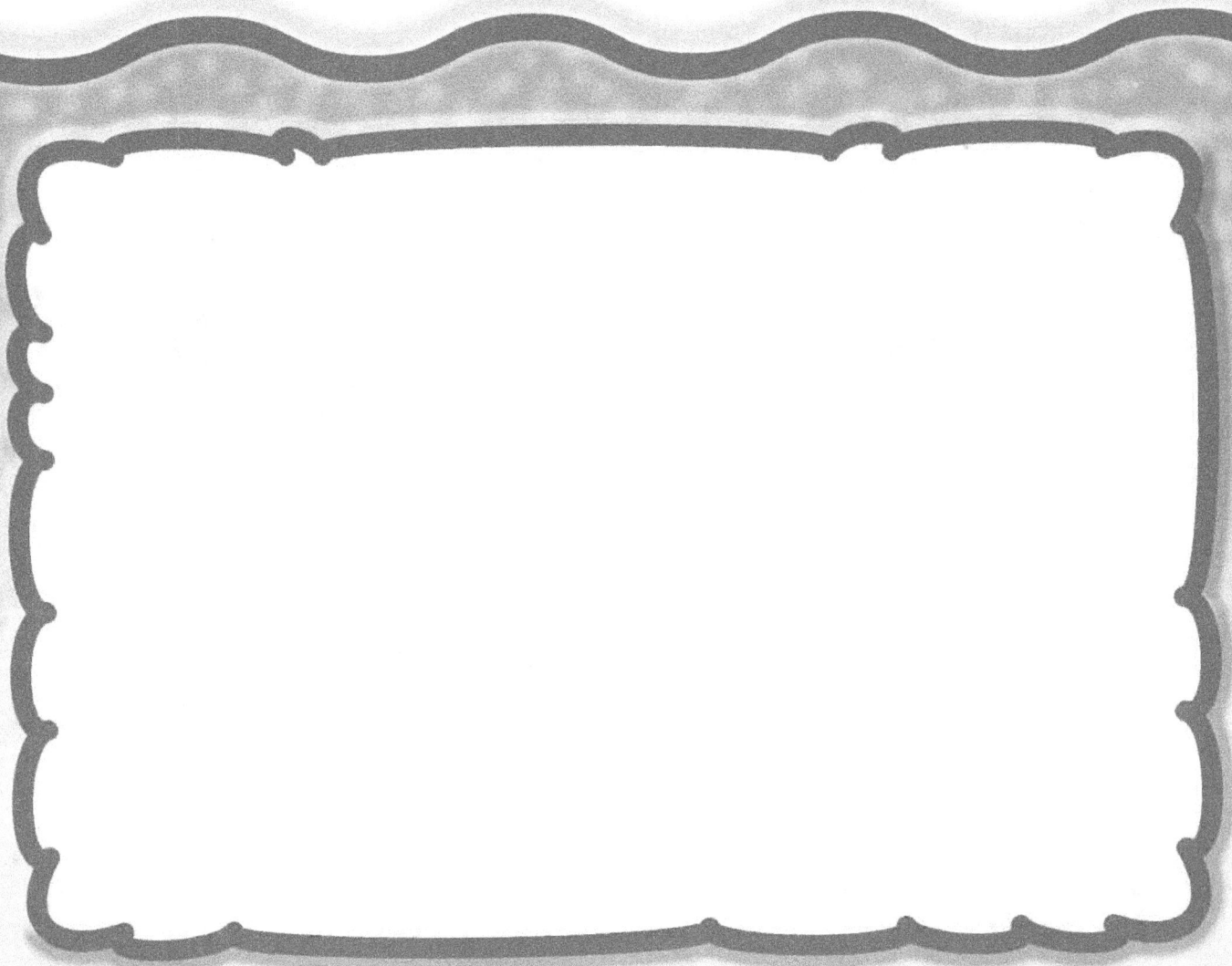

ADAM AND EVE DISOBEY GOD

God saw all that he had made, and it was very good. (Genesis 1:31).

God is our Creator

¡Oh-oh!

MY NAME:

43

Dear Parents: Adam and Eve disobeyed God; they made a bad decision, but God still loved them. Today your child learned that when people make bad decisions, that always brings bad consequences. Although sometimes we do wrong, God continues to love us. Talk with your child about how Adam and Eve disobeyed their Creator. Then, help them paste the figures, which are found in the Cut-Out Section, in the correct order into the boxes below according to the Bible story. Help your child think about how they can make right decisions and obey God.

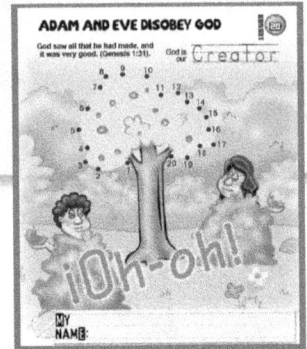

God is
our
Creator

Disobedience to God ...

1   2   3

... I will obey God!

NOAH OBEYS GOD

2 by 2

God is our Creator

God made everything that exists.

God told Noah to build an ark. When it was ready, the animals entered 2 by 2. Draw a line from each animal on the left to the matching animal on the right.

MY NAME:

Everyone to the ark!

God is
our   Creator

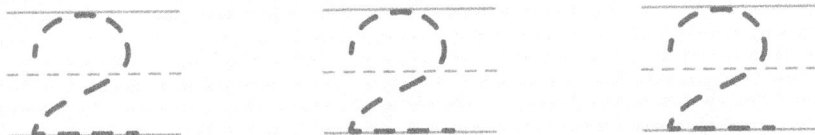

How did the animals enter the ark? (2 by 2)

GOD MAKES A
Promise
to Abraham

MY NAME:

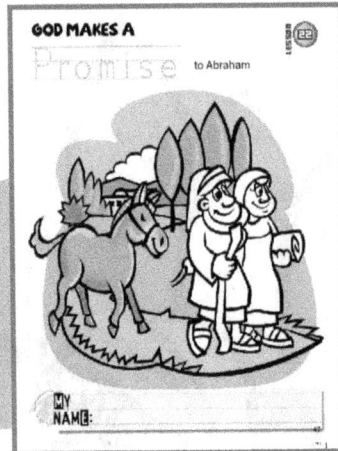

GOD MAKES A

Promise to Abraham

MY NAME:

God keeps his Promise to Abraham

Dear Parents:

The lessons of this unit will help children understand that God always keeps his promises. The Word of Faith for this unit is "Promise." A promise is to be kept. Explain to your child that we should trust in God because He always keeps His promises.

LOT MAKES A DECISION

MY
NAME:

I CAN DECIDE!

Lot made a decision. You also can decide. Make a drawing of something that you can decide to do at home.

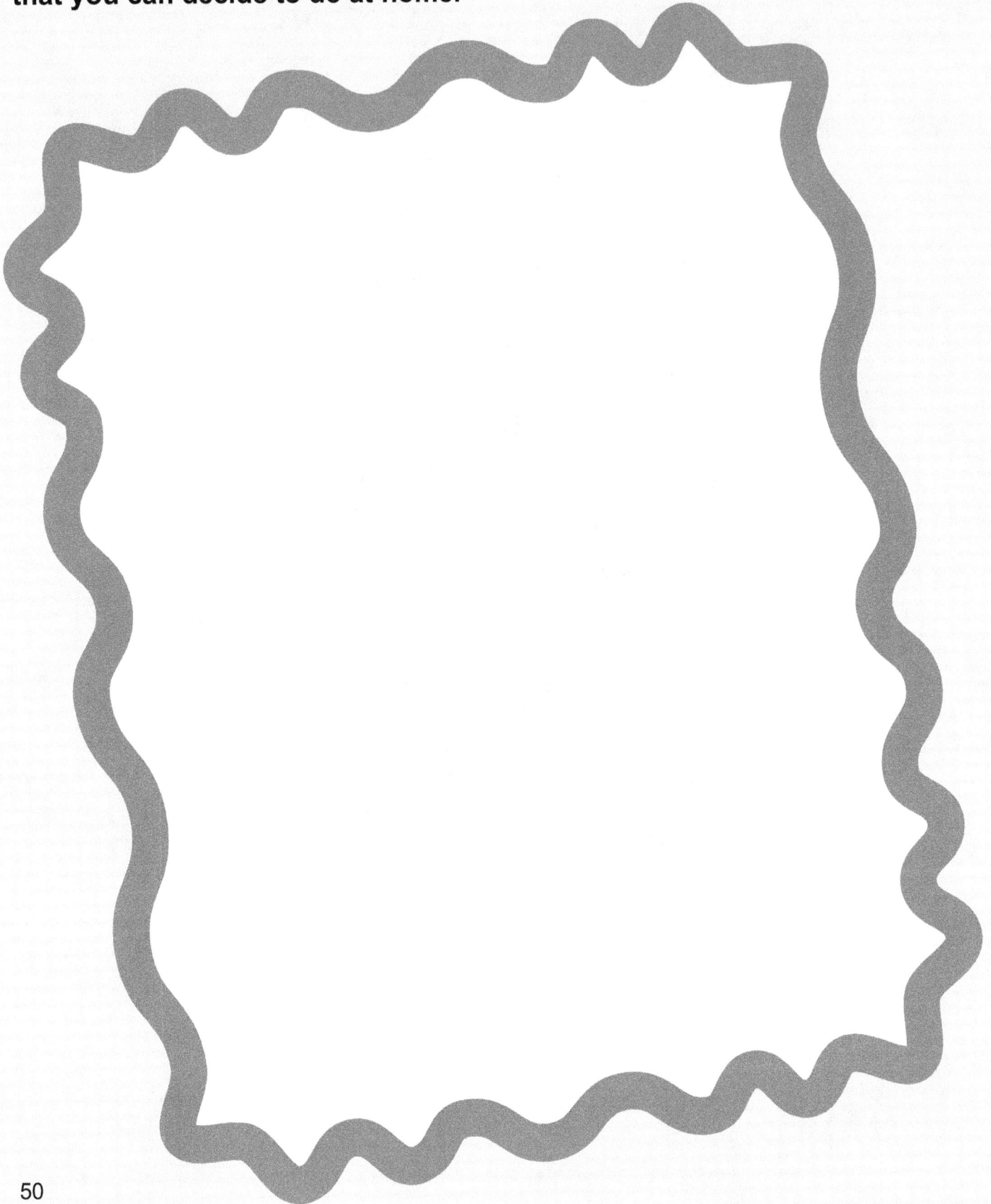

God
keeps
His

Promise

that he made to Abraham

MY
NAME:

God
keeps
His
Promise
that he made to Abraham

MY NAME:

Dear Parents

Today's lesson is: "God keeps his promise that He made to Abraham." Tell your child that God also keeps the promises that he makes to your family. Help your child glue or tape a photo or drawing of your family in the entrance of the tent.

THE BIRTH OF ISAAC

MY NAME:

God keeps his Promises

Dear Parents

Today we celebrated the fulfillment of the promise that God made to Abraham: the birth of his son Isaac. Have your child glue or tape a photo of a baby in the picture frame below, or they can draw a picture of a baby.

ELIEZER FINDS A WIFE FOR ISAAC

MY NAME:

God keeps his Promises

Jacob Loves **his son Joseph**

Color in with red the letters that do not have a dot to find the hidden word.

MY NAME:

God wants families to show Love

The lessons of this unit will help your child understand that God wants families to love and take care of each other. God loves everyone equally. The Bible stories of this unit tell us about Joseph's family. Talk with your child about God's love. Encourage your family to love in the same way that God loves us.

Instructions: Make copies of the rectangle below. Your students can color them and use them to write letters to family members and express how much they love them; or they can give them away to be used as bookmarks.

Love

JOSEPH FINDS HIS BROTHERS

MY
NAME:

Instructions: Look in the Cut-Out Section for the picture of Joseph's brothers. The children can then glue or tape the picture at the exit of the maze. Then they can try to find the shortest way from Joseph to his brothers. There are three distinct ways. They can trace the different routes with different colors.

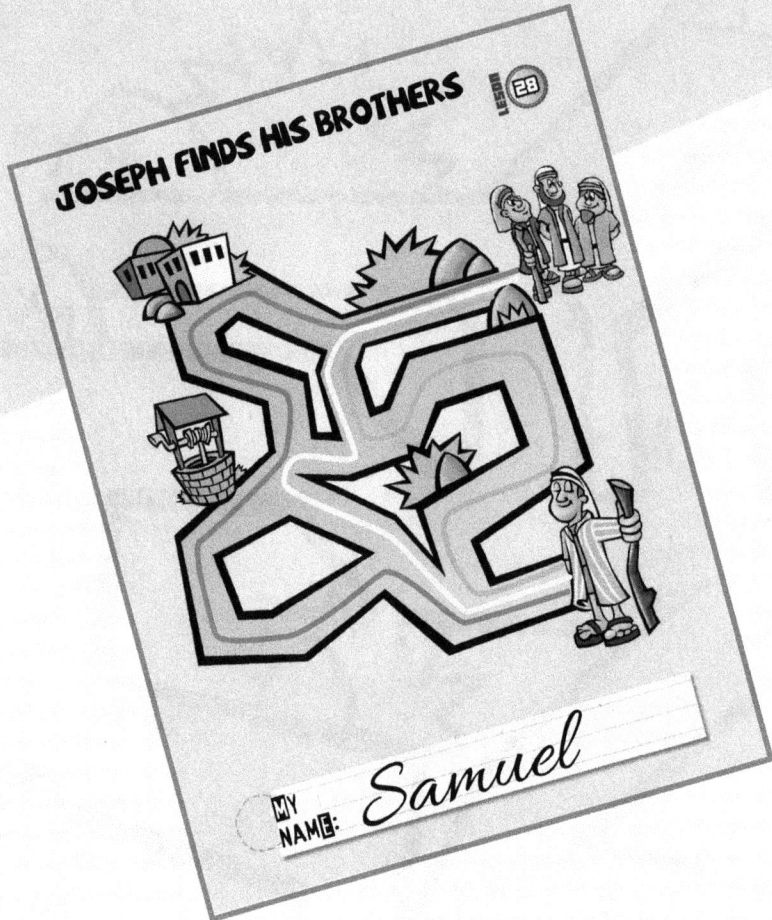

JOSEPH FINDS HIS BROTHERS

LESSON 28

MY NAME: Samuel

JOSEPH HELPS HIS FAMILY

MY
NAME:

JOSEPH HELPS HIS FAMILY

LESSON 29

MY NAME:

Instructions: Students who wish may paste their activity sheet on construction paper or cardboard.

Jacob Loves his grandchildren.

MY
NAME:

Our FAMILY

Instructions: Have the children draw a picture of different family members in each box. Help your
students know that God wants families to love and care for each other.

GOD PROTECTS MOSES

The Lord is good ...

He takes good care of

those who trust in him.

(Nahum 1:7)

Baby Moses

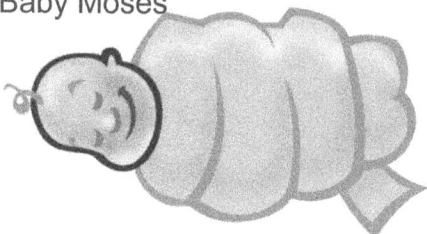

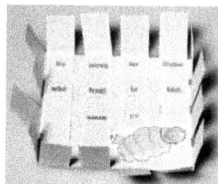

Carefully cut out the eight strips of paper above and the figure of baby Moses. Help the children place four strips vertically on the table. Then arrange the remaining strips horizontally, as shown in the example. Glue the strips together, forming a basket, leaving the text on top. Now it's time to put the baby Moses in the finished basket.

Dear Parents: Today we learned about the baby that was put in a basket. It was Moses. God cared for him, just as He cares for us. Encourage your child by telling the Bible story of baby Moses during this week (Exodus 2:1-10).

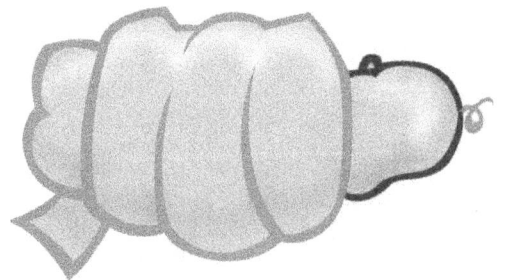

MOSES OBEYS GOD

The Lord is good ... He takes good care of those who trust in him. (Nahum 1:7).

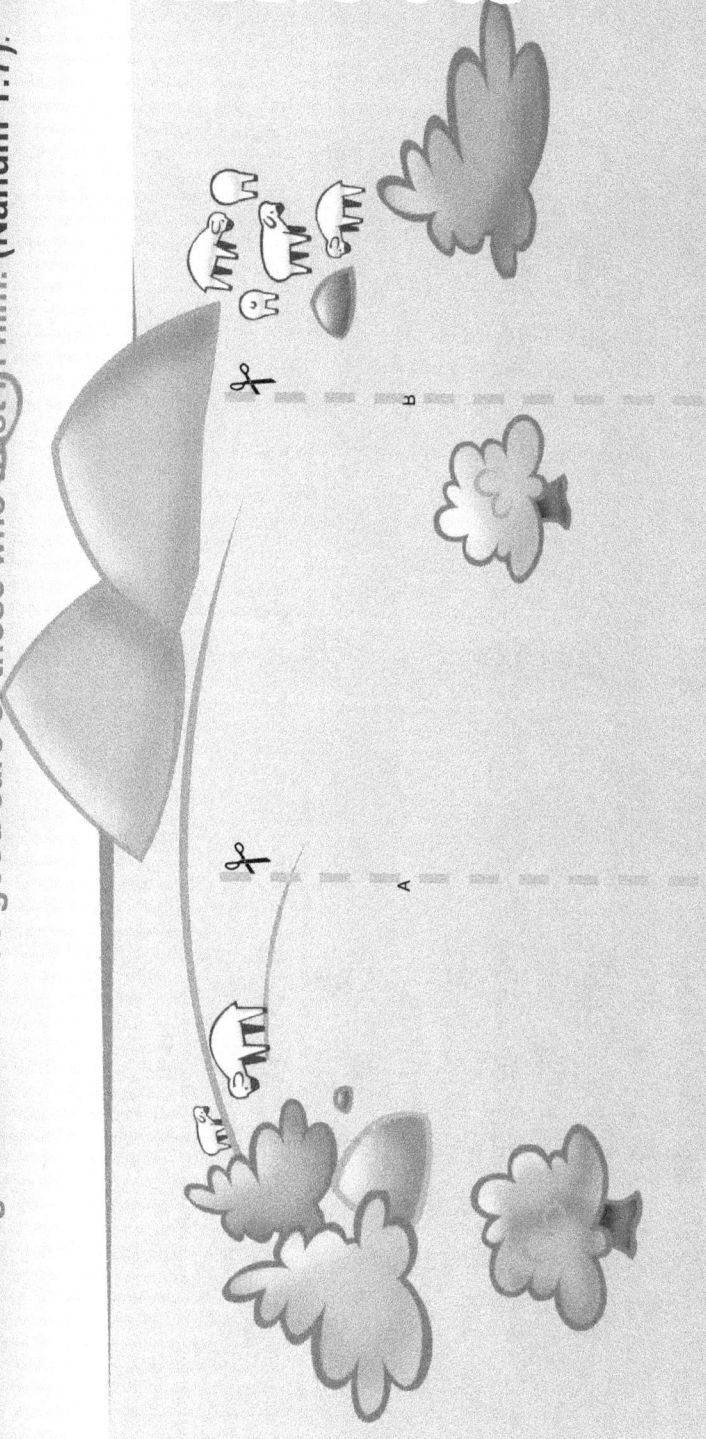

Moses obeys God. I also want to obey God.

Figure 1 ↑

Figure 2 ↑

Instructions: Cut out the desert scene and the strip on the right with the drawings of Moses by the fire. Make cuts vertically where indicated in the desert scene.

Help the children to:

1. Insert the strip of drawings through the slits in the desert scene, as the example shows.

2. Remind the children of the Bible story while the children move the drawing strip, showing Figure 1 first and then 2.

4. Talk to them about ways in which they can obey God. **Explain that God took care of Moses because he obeyed Him. We can also obey God. He is happy when we obey Him.**

67

Dear Parents:

Encourage your child to tell you the Bible story about "Moses and the burning bush" (Exodus 3:1-12). Moses obeyed God and we also should do the same thing. Talk with him/her about the importance of obeying God and how it makes God happy when we obey Him.

MOSES TRUSTS IN GOD

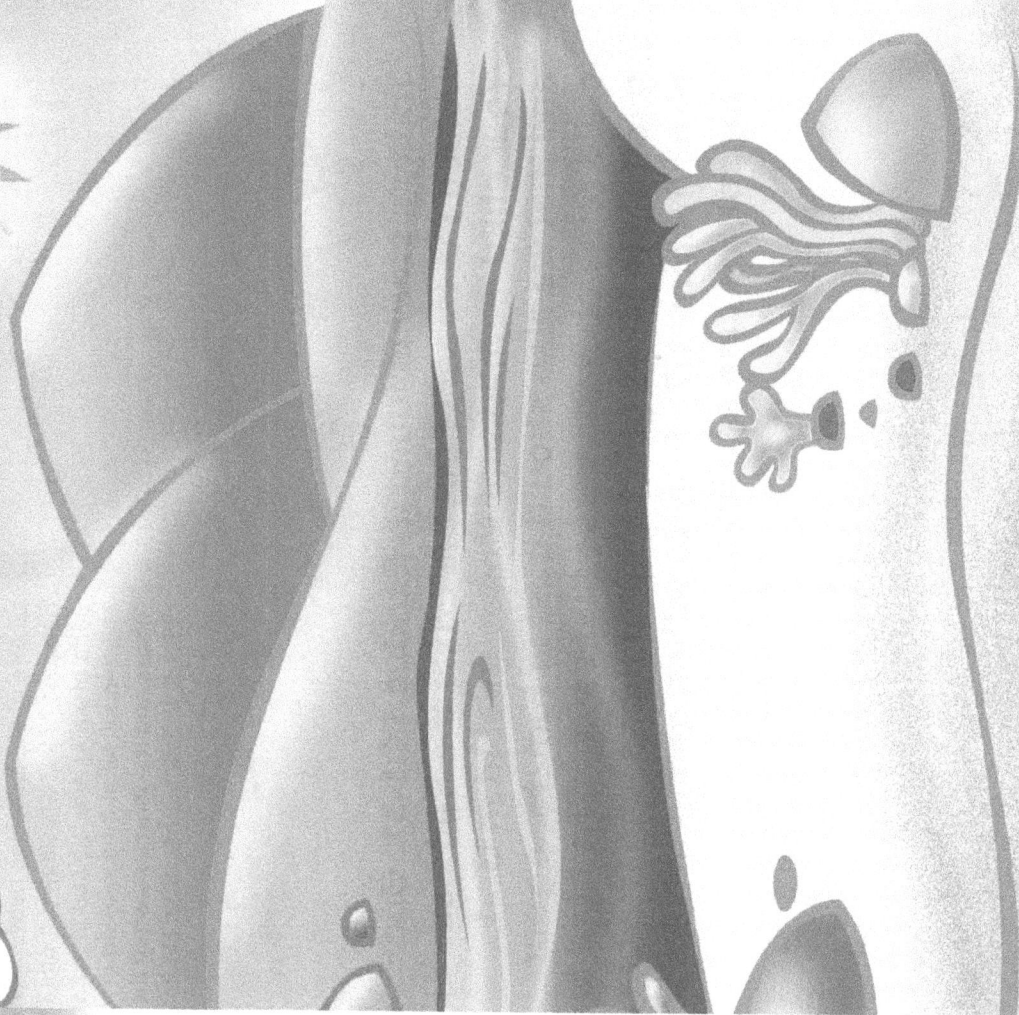
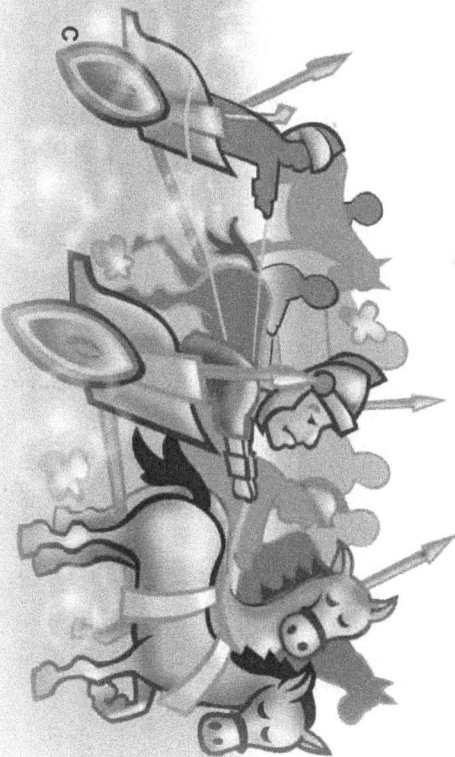

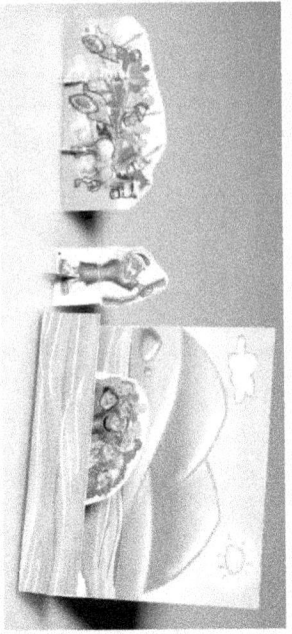

Instructions: If you had to copy the worksheet for the children, you can first have them color everything, including the picture of the water below the parent note. Cut out the figures of Moses, the Israelites, the Egyptian army, and the cut out bases. Each figure must be glued to the cutout bases to help them stand. Help the children with this task. Then, fold the bottom of the page so the sea picture on this page can be seen in front of the other picture of the mountains and the sea. Then place the picture of the Israelites between the two water sections (see example to the left) to represent the passage of the Israelites through the Red Sea. Later, you can take the Israelites out from the two parts of water and replace them with the Egyptian army and cover the army with the water. Let the children tell what they learned in the biblical story using the figures. Remind them that God helped Moses and the Israelites when they fled from Pharaoh. We can also trust that God will help us in difficult situations, because He loves us and cares for us

Dear Parents:

Today's story is found in Exodus 14:1-31. God helped the Israelite people cross the Red Sea. Your child learned that Moses trusted in God, and that we also should trust in Him. Help your child remember the verse that says, "The Lord is good ... He takes good care of those who trust in him" (Nahum 1:7). Pray together, giving thanks to God for His care and love.

MOSES TEACHES THE PEOPLE TO TRUST IN GOD

Instructions: Carefully cut out the 6 cards and put them on a table, with the drawings of the people facing down. One by one, the children will take turns picking up two cards, trying to make a match. Once all of the matches are made, they can retell the story by arranging the cards in order.

Dear Parents: Ask your child to show you what they learned in class today, using the memorization game. Ask them questions about the story of Exodus 15:22-27, when the people of Israel found the bitter water.

GOD PROVIDES FOOD FOR HIS PEOPLE

The Lord is good...
He takes good care
of those who trust in
him (Nahum 1:7).

Thank you God, for
your love and care.

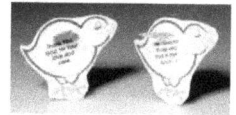

Instructions: Cut out the figures of the wings and the quail. Have the children color the birds. Carefully, make a horizontal cut above the text on the line, then the children can insert the wings through the cuts (see the example). They can glue the birds to popsicle sticks and then carry them around as they "fly" the birds. If you want, as a class go around the class flying your birds as the class repeats the memory verse.

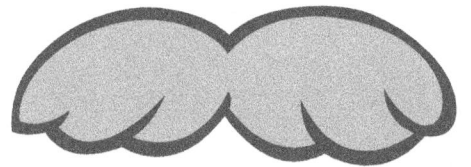

JEHOSEPHAT SENDS TEACHERS WITH THE WORD OF GOD

The **Bible**

is a special book.

Jehoshaphat obeys
the Word of God.

I will obey your Word.

(Psalm 119:17)

MY
NAME:

Jehoshaphat's Scroll

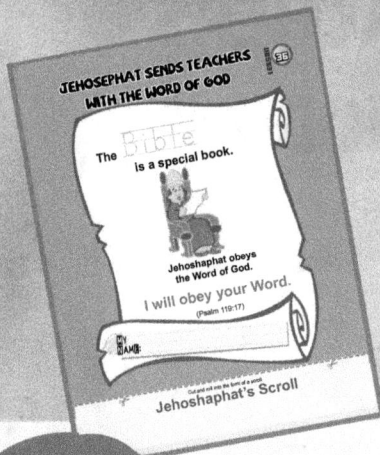

JEHOSEPHAT SENDS TEACHERS
WITH THE WORD OF GOD

The **Bible** is a special book.

Jehoshaphat obeys
the Word of God.

I will obey your Word.
(Psalm 119:17)

Jehoshaphat's Scroll

Dear Parents: Our Word of Faith for the following 4 weeks is: Bible. This beautiful word will help your child understand better the significance of the Word of God. We celebrate that the Bible is a special book that speaks to us about God, and helps us know him better. Use this word when you talk with your child. Talk to him/her about their favorite Bible Stories.

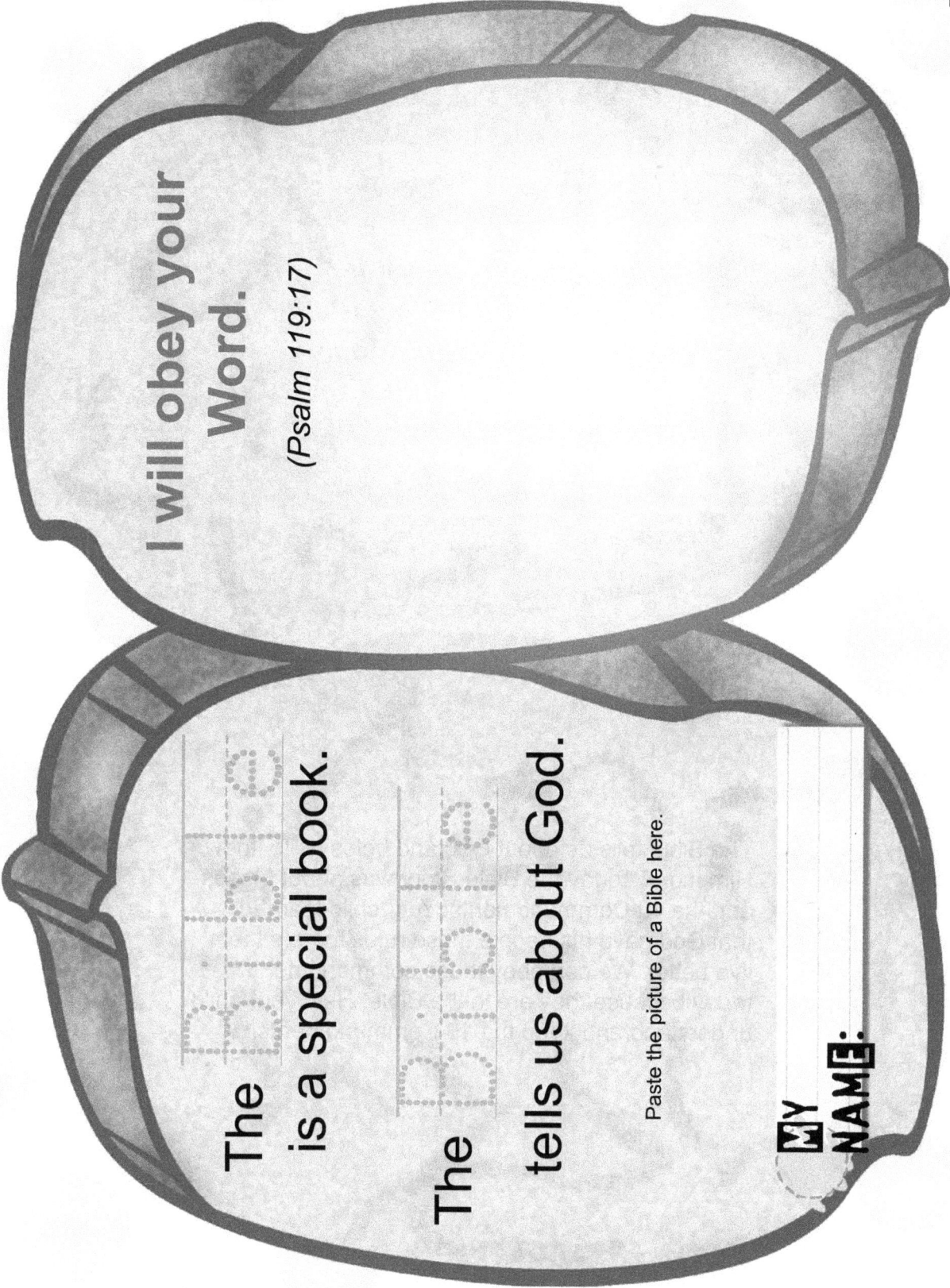

I will obey your Word.

(Psalm 119:17)

The B i b l e is a special book.

The B i b l e tells us about God.

Paste the picture of a Bible here.

MY NAME:

Only for Children

1. Tell your favorite Bible Story to someone you love very much.
2. Next, tell the story of Moses and the Commandments that God gave him on the mountain.

Dear Parents:

The Bible tells us about God and helps us to know Him more. Today the Bible Story was about Moses and the 10 Commandments. Your child learned that God gave his people these rules to help them live better. We can obey those commandments today because they are in the Bible. Help your child understand and keep the 10 Commandments.

The **Bible** is a special book that tells us about God.

How many scrolls can you find in this destroyed temple?

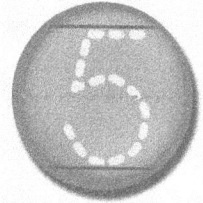

How many scrolls were found by King Josia's helpers?

5

MY NAME:

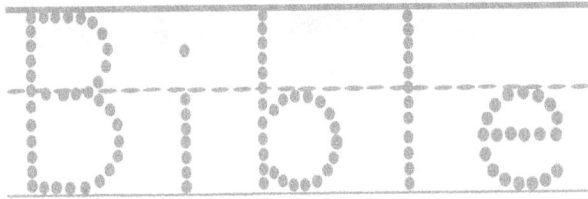

The **Bible** is a special book.

Draw a picture of your Bible.

The **Bible**

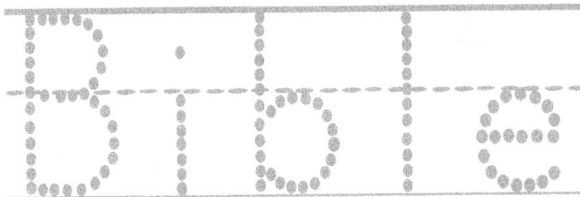

tells us about God and helps us know Him.

Dear Parents:

Today your child learned that King Josiah loved God and wanted to obey Him (2 Chronicles 34:14-33). Ask your child how it was that the King's helpers found the Word of God in the temple. Repeat together the memory verse: "I will obey your Word (Psalms 119:17).

JEREMIAH PROCLAIMS THE WORD OF GOD

The **Bible**

is a special book.

I will obey your Word.

MY NAME:

What special book helps you to know God?

BIBLE

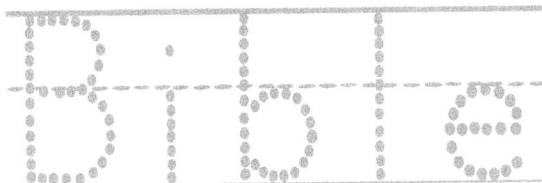

The **Bible** tells us about God.

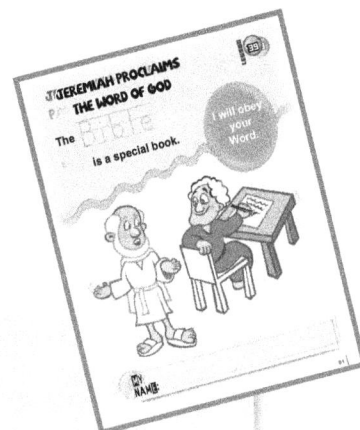

THE POWER OF GOD IN JERICHO

A

B

Paste to B.

THE WALLS FALL

Great is our
Lord and
mighty in
power

(Psalm 147:5)

fold

double

fold

God is
great and
powerful.

3

1

1

2

2

God has
great **Power**

3

MY
NAME:

God has great Power

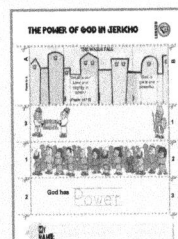

God has
great Power

THE POWER OF GOD WHEN IT DOESN'T RAIN

Great is our Lord and mighty in power (Psalm 147:5).

God has great

power

MY NAME:

Dear Parents:

Our Word of Faith for this unit is **"Power."** We have learned that the power of God is immense. God used it to help Elijah. Explain to your child that God showed his power to Elijah because he loved and obeyed God. Review the Bible Story with your child, using the illustration to the right. You can read the words while your child names the figures.

Figure 1: Elijah; figure 2: crows; figure 3: Elijah; figure 4: Elijah; figure 5: sun; figure 6: rain

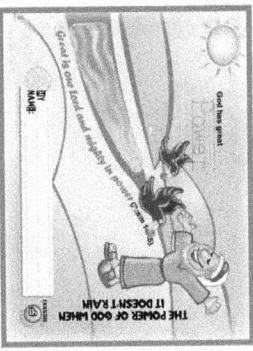

THE POWER OF GOD WHEN IT DOESN'T RAIN

God is our Lord and Ability to provide Grace to us

God has great

God gave food to

God took care of

God showed his love to

when the

burned hotly and there was no

by sending some

God has great

Power

THE POWER OF GOD ON MOUNT CARMEL

God sends fire

God has great

Power

MY NAME:

Great **is** **our**

and

God **Great**

is His

Dear Parents:

POUVWA BONDYE SOU
MÒN KAMÈL LA

Bondye
voye dife

Bondye gen
Pouvwa

OVER
RELB *Ana*

Today your child learned about how God helped Elijah defeat the prophets of Baal. God sent fire from heaven to burn up the altar that Elijah had prepared, and all the people believed in the incredible power of God (1 Kings 18:16-39). Point out each flame of fire and repeat with your child each word of the memory verse. Help him/her to trace the Word of Faith, and explain to them that the power of God is infinite and there is nothing that compares to it in the world.

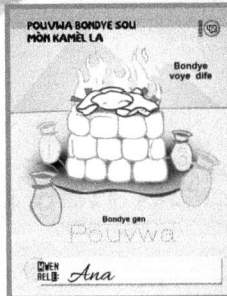

Power

(Psalm 147:5)

THE POWER OF GOD IN THE FIERY FURNACE

MY NAME:

1 2 3 4

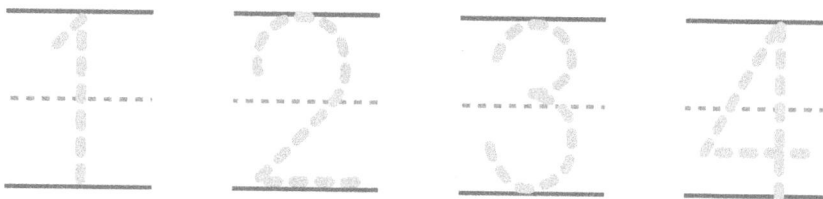

Great is our Lord and mighty in power (Psalm 147:5).

God has great Power

Circle the figures that you think can not withstand the fire. Remember that Shadrach, Meshach and Abednego survived the blazing flames because God protected them. God is more powerful than anything.

90

THE POWER OF GOD WITH DANIEL IN THE LIONS DEN

God has great Power

MY NAME:

91

God used His great

Power

to save Daniel!

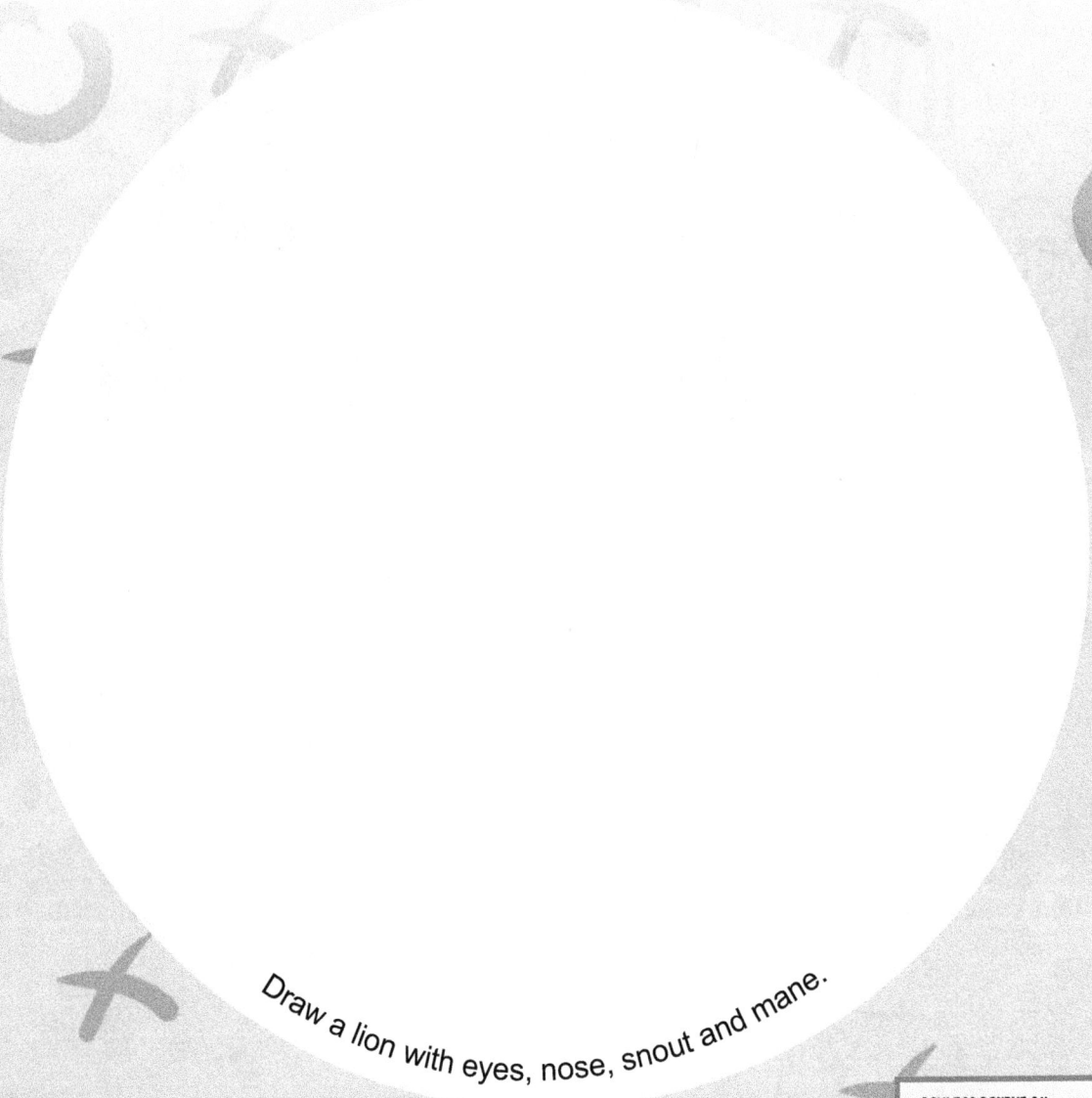

Draw a lion with eyes, nose, snout and mane.

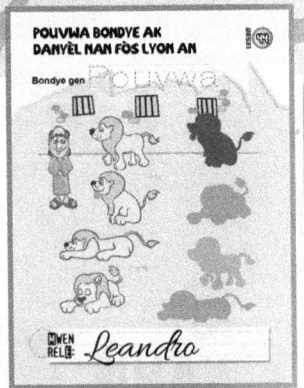

POUVWA BONDYE AK
DANYÈL NAN FÒS LYON AN

Bondye gen

Pouvwa

OWEN
RELE: *Leandro*

PETER TALKS ABOUT JESUS

A disciple of

Jesus

is someone
who loves him
and tells others
about him.

They never stopped teaching and proclaiming the good news that Jesus is the Messiah (Acts 5:42).

MY
NAME:

Who was the disciple of Jesus **in our Bible Story today?**

A M F I T P W I
K E N B M Z T X
Q L Z E U W R F

Color the letters with the dot and find the hidden name. Color the other letters with different colors.

We can also be disciples!

PETER TALKS ABOUT JESUS

A disciple of Jesus is someone who loves him and tells others about him.

They never stopped teaching and proclaiming the good news that Jesus is the Messiah (Acts 5:42)

MY NAME:

Dear Parents:

Today your child met a new Bible character: the disciple Peter. The Word of Faith for this unit is **"disciple."** During the following lessons, your child will learn what it means to be a disciple of Christ through stories about Peter's life. Talk with your child about what it means to follow Jesus. Explain that a disciple is someone who loves Jesus and speaks to others about Him.

PETER HELPS A LAME MAN

Peter was a disciple of

They never stopped teaching and proclaiming the good news that Jesus is the Messiah (Acts 5:42).

Jesus

MY NAME:

A **disciple of** Jesus **is someone who loves him and tells others about him.**

Draw yourself. Look at your face in the mirror. What do you see? You are someone important to Jesus. He loves you! And just like Peter, you can speak to others about your friend Jesus.

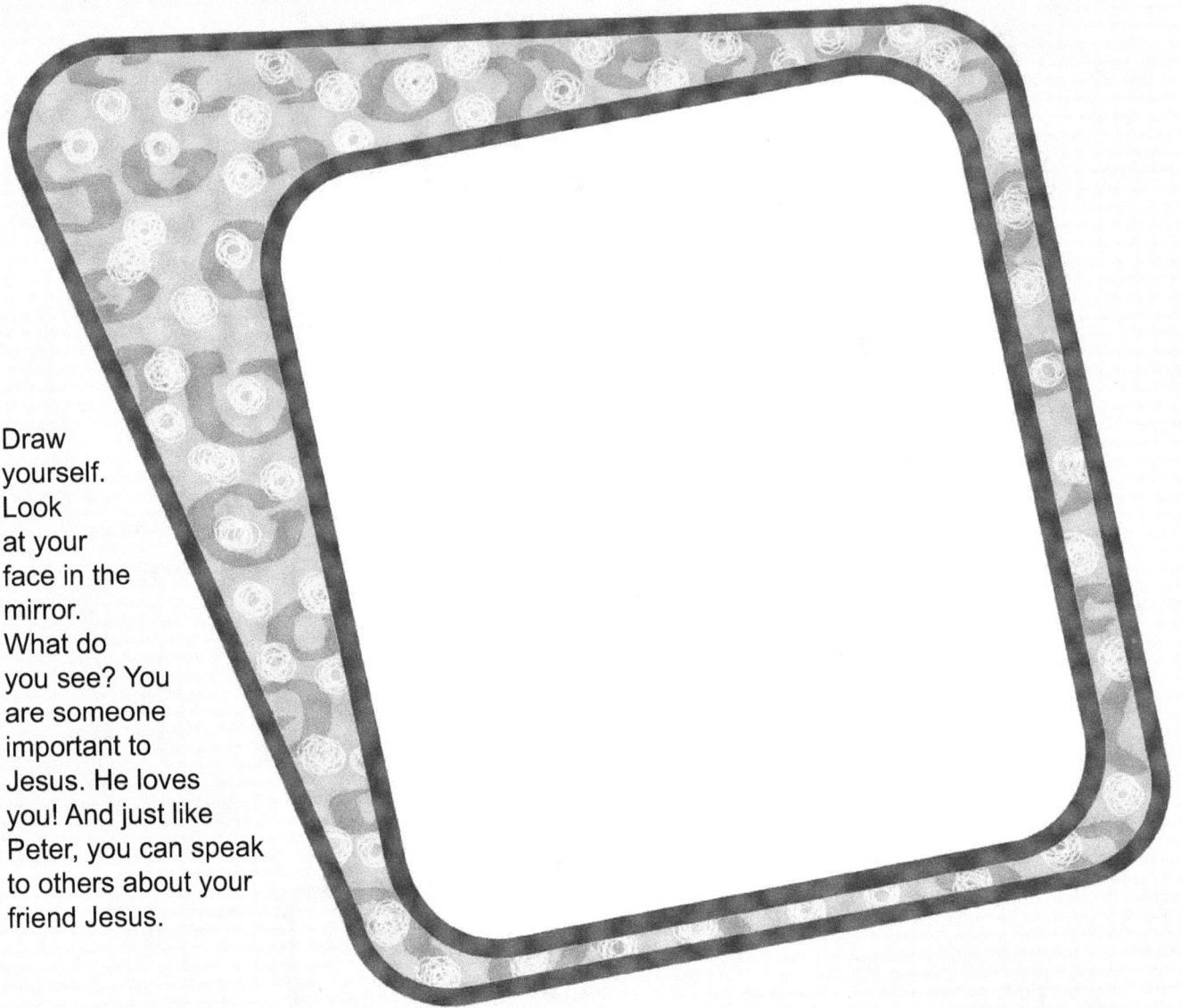

Dear Parents:

Today your child studied how Peter healed a man that couldn't walk, and Peter also shared the gospel with him. Peter was Jesus' disciple and wanted to tell others about the Messiah. Ask your child to tell you about the Bible story of today: "Peter heals a paralytic at the temple gate." (Acts 3:1-10).

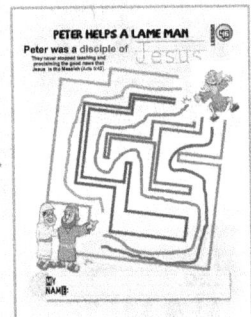

A disciple of *Jesus* **is someone who loves Jesus and tells others about Him.**

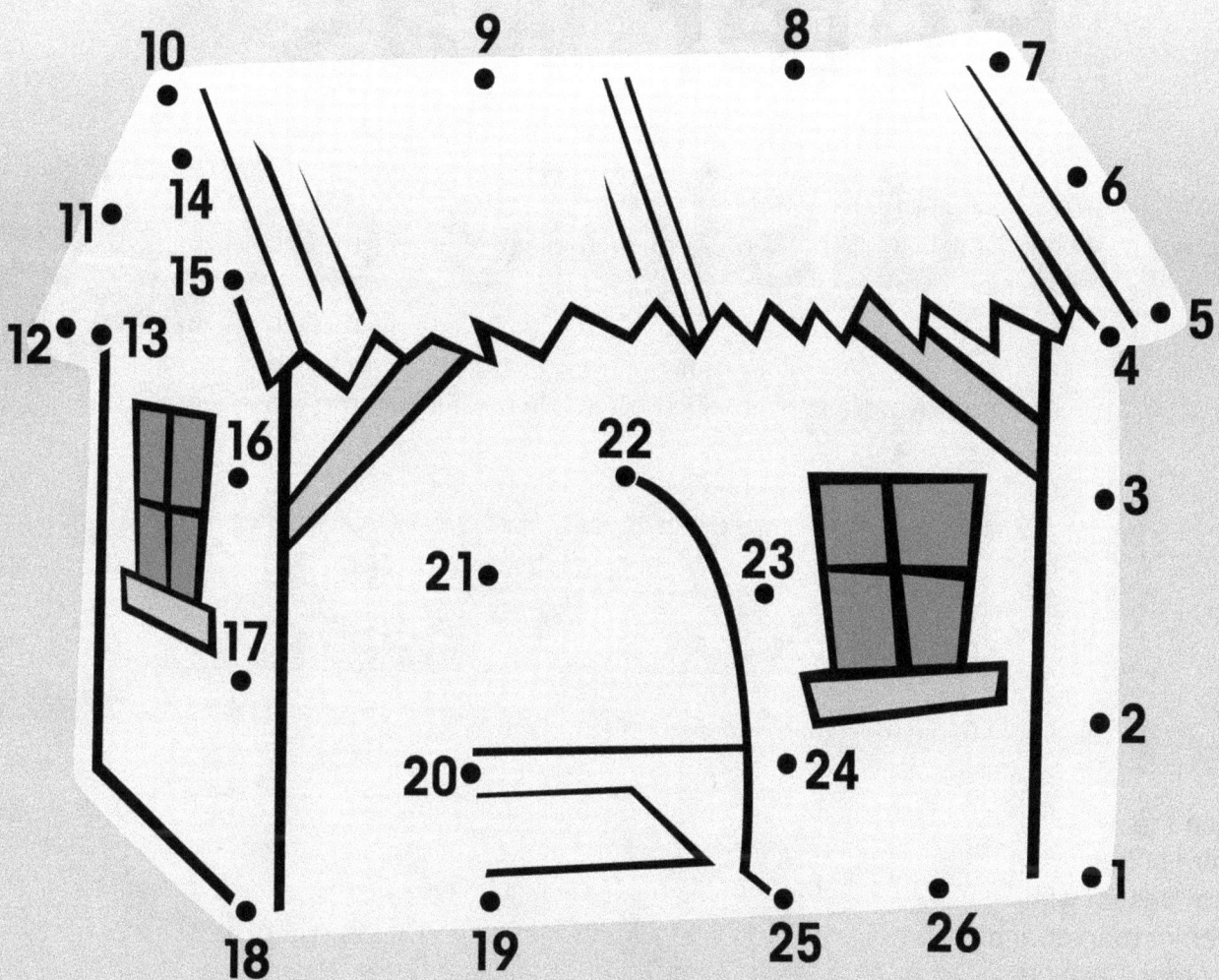

10 9 8 7
14
11 6
15
12 13 5
4
16 22
3
21 23
17 2
20 24
1
18 19 25 26

They never stopped teaching and proclaiming the good news that Jesus is the Messiah.
(Acts 5:42)

MY NAME:

Peter was a disiple of

Jesus

Trace the letters of the word "Jesus" with a pen or marker and decorate it as you would like.

Dear Parents:

Today your child learned that Jesus' love is for everyone. Ask your child to tell you the Bible Story we studied today: "Peter visits a captain of 100 soldiers named Cornelius" (Acts 10:1-2, 17-24, 28, 34-36).

PETER'S FRIENDS PRAY FOR HIM

1 Peter was Jesus' disciple.

4 Peter was reunited with his friends.

They never stopped teaching and proclaiming the good news that Jesus is the Messiah.
(Acts 5:24)

Peter in jail

2 Peter's friends prayed for him.

3 God sent an angel to free Peter.

Cut out and glue to page 1 of this booklet.

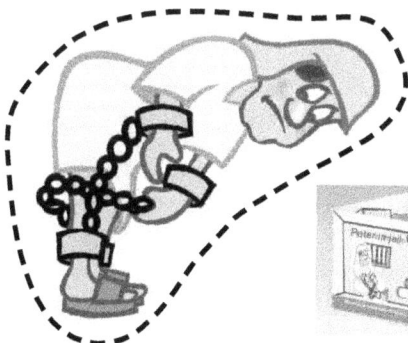

Cut out the scene along solid lines, and fold it along the dotted lines to form a little book (see example). Cut out the figures, and have the children put them in the correct place according to the Bible story. They can color it if they wish.

Cut out and glue the figure onto page 3 of the booklet.

99

Fold here

Fold here

This is how God showed his love to us: He sent his one and only son Jesus into the world (1 John 4:9)

Fold backwards

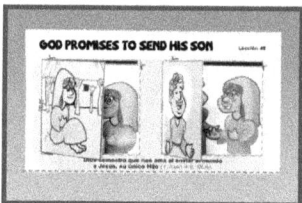

Instructions: Cut around three sides of the boxes above along the dotted lines. Then fold along the solid line. Fold up the page along the dotted line, so that the figures on the back side of the page show through the windows when the figures are folded outward. Help the students remember the Bible story using the pictures. Invite them to color the pictures. While doing this activity, review the memory verse.

Dear Parents:

Today your child learned about the celebration of Jesus' birth. We studied that God promised to send his Son Jesus, the Messiah. We celebrate his birth at Christmas. The Bible story told us about the visit that the angel Gabriel made to Mary to give her good news from God. She would be the mother of the only Son of God (Luke 1: 26-35, 38). During this week, talk with your child about God's love, and prepare him/her for the joy that Christmas brings.

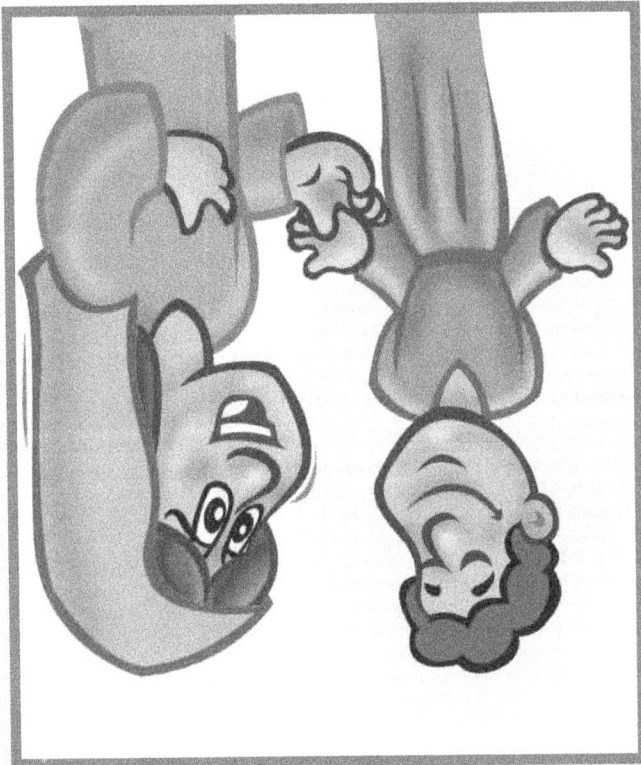 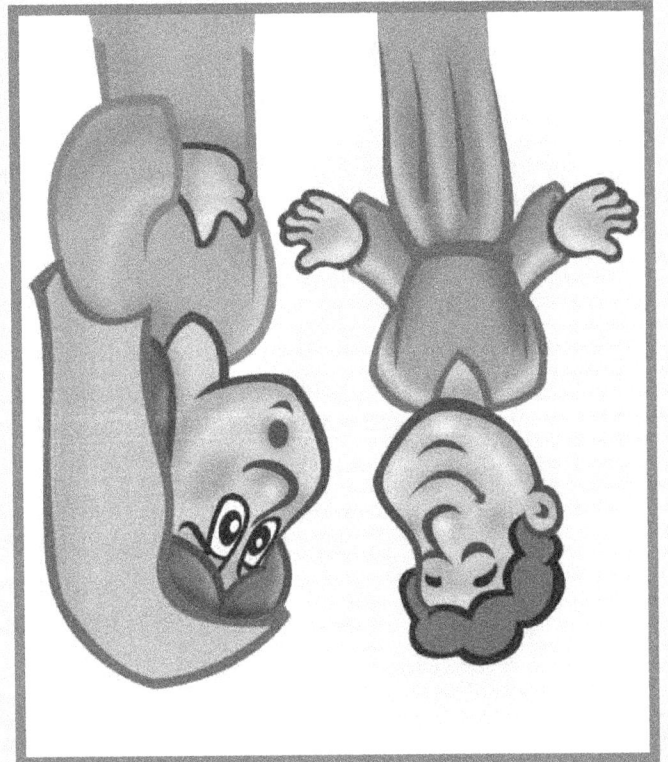

GOD SENDS HIS SON

This is how God showed his love to us: He sent his one and only son Jesus into the world.
(1 John 4:9)

Jesus is the son of God.

Name:

GOD SENDS HIS SON

Instructions: Help your students cut out both circles. Put one on top of the other, taking care that they are well aligned. The circle with the Bible verse must go on top of the one with the figures. Then connect them through the center with a paper fastener. Encourage the children to rotate the upper circle, and remember the Bible story using the drawings.

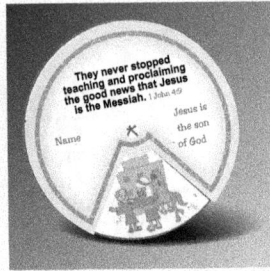

Take note, you will need a paper fastener for each child.

Dear Parents:
Today your child learned about Joseph and Mary's journey to Bethlehem and Jesus' birth in the stable (Luke 21:1-7, 21). Tell your child that God loves them so much. That's why God sent Jesus, His only son. Remind them that Christmas is a special time that we celebrate and give thanks to God for Jesus' birth.

THE SHEPHERDS GO TO SEE JESUS

We celebrate
Jesus, the son
of God.

Name:

Instructions: Provide your students with figures of angels, shepherds and sheep from the Cut Out section. Tell them to color and cut them out. Then hand out the activity sheets and glue. Invite the children to reconstruct the Bible story, while placing the figures on the way to Bethlehem. Use the pictures that the children glue on the page, and ask them about the content of the story. For example: According to what we learned today, what did the shepherds do? (They left their sheep and went to look for the baby Jesus. They were very excited about what the angels had told them.)

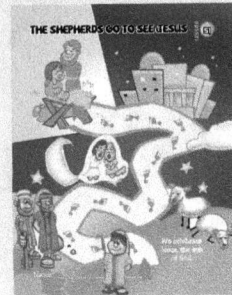

Dear Parents:

Today your child learned about the joy of the shepherds when they heard the good news of the birth of the Messiah. They were so excited about what the angels had said that they went running to look for the baby Jesus (Luke 2:8-20). This week, celebrate Christmas with your child. Make a cake for Jesus and invite your child's friends to celebrate His birth. Remember to tell them the good news that Jesus is the Son of God!

We give thanks to God for Jesus!

fold

Simeon and Anna give thanks to God!

SIMEON AND ANNA SEE THE SON OF GOD

Dear Parents:

In this lesson, we learned how Simeon and Anna worshiped God because of His Son Jesus (Luke 2:21-38). While you celebrate Christmas with your child, express through your words and actions your worship to God for the gift that He gave us through Jesus Christ. Merry Christmas!

Instructions: Give the children the activity worksheet. Help them remember the Bible Story while they look at the picture of Simeon and Anna in the temple with the baby Jesus. Have them cut along the dotted lines around the picture, creating a window. Then, fold the worksheet in half. When they open the windows, they will see the Bible verse on the reverse side of the windows. Say the verse with the group. Encourage them to give thanks to God, just as Anna and Simeon did. Invite them to draw a picture of how they would like to thank God for his Son Jesus, which they will be able to see through the windows.

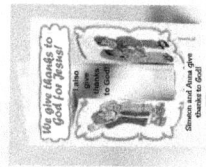

This is
how God
showed his
love to us:
He sent his
one and
only son
Jesus into
the world.

1 John 4:9

I also give thanks to God!

110

Lesson 40

Cut Out
Section

Lesson 37

Lesson 43

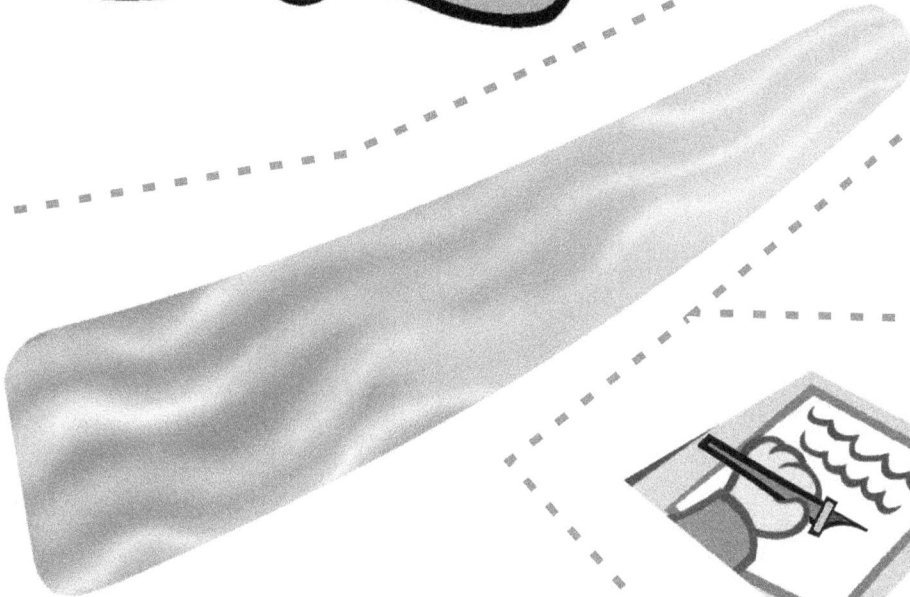

Lesson 39

Jehoshaphat

Lesson 41

Lesson 36

Lesson 22

Timothy

Lesson 10

Lesson 10

Lesson 10

Lesson 24

Lesson 23

113

Lesson 16

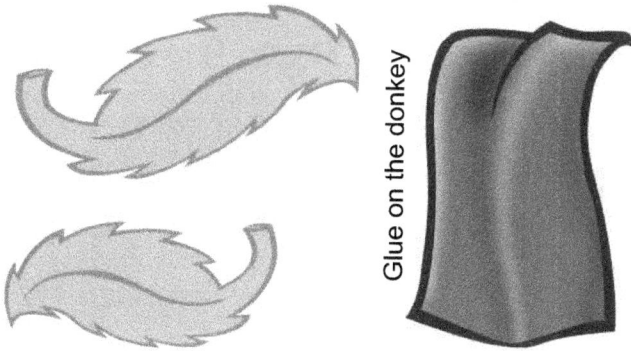

Glue on the donkey

Lesson 5

Lesson 8

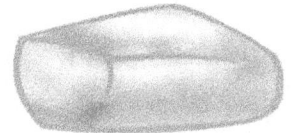

Lesson 8

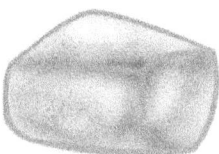

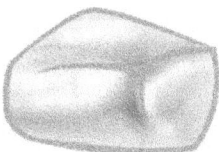

Cut out the 12 loaves of bread and glue them in the 12 baskets.

115

Additional
Pictures

My command is
this: Love each
other as I have
loved you.
(John 15:12)

Unit III

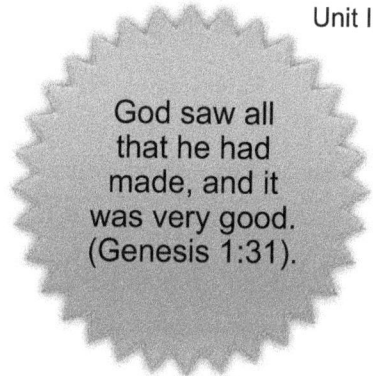

God saw all
that he had
made, and it
was very good.
(Genesis 1:31).

Unit V

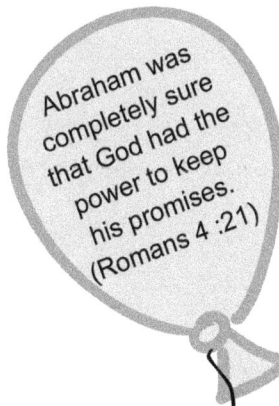

Abraham was
completely sure
that God had the
power to keep
his promises.
(Romans 4 :21)

Unit VI

Lesson 51

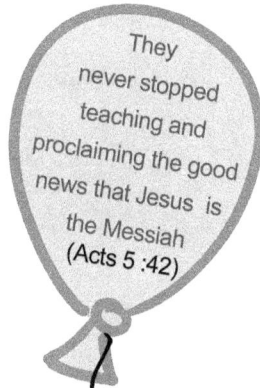

They never stopped teaching and proclaiming the good news that Jesus is the Messiah (Acts 5 :42)

Unit XI

This is how God showed his love to us: He sent his one and only son Jesus into the world. (1 J 4 :9)

Unit XII

Lesson 4

Lesson 3

Lesson 2

Lesson 1

Lesson 19

Additional
Pictures

Lesson 17

Jesus Lives!

Celebrate!

Lesson 20

Lesson 28

Lesson 29

Unit I

Unit II

Give all your worries to God, because he cares for you.

(1 Peter 5:7).

And the child grew and became strong.

(Lik 2 :40)

Lesson 25

Rebecca

Lesson 26

Unit VII

A new command I give you: Love one another. As I have loved you,

(John 13:34).

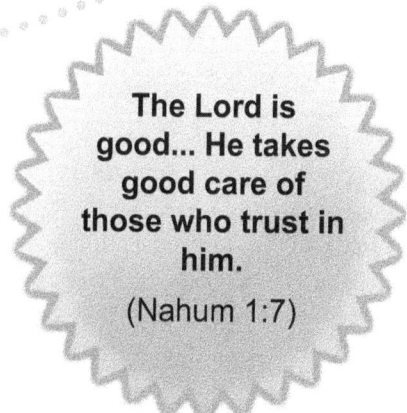

The Lord is good... He takes good care of those who trust in him.

(Nahum 1:7)

Peter

Lesson 45

You are the Messiah, the Son of the living God.
(Matthew 16:16).

The lame man

Lesson 46

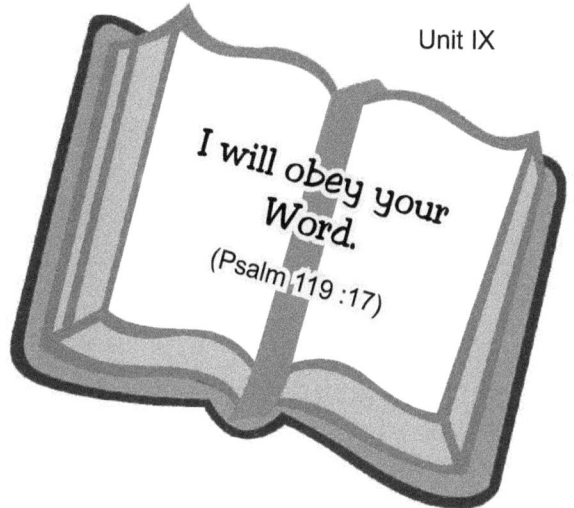

I will obey your Word.
(Psalm 119 :17)

Peter and Cornelius

Lesson 47

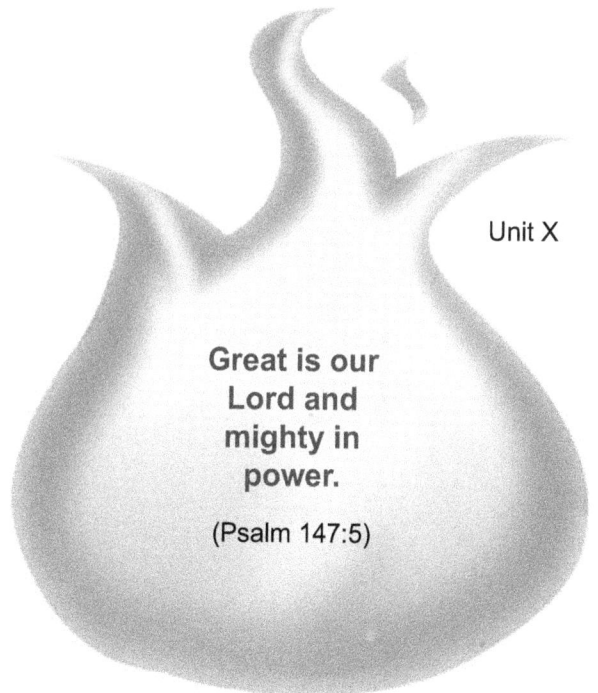

Great is our Lord and mighty in power.
(Psalm 147:5)